VINTAGE BLUEBELL

THE EARLY YEARS [illegible]OUR

Published by Runpast Publishing, 10 Kingscote Grove, Cheltenham, Gloucestershire GL51 6JX.

ISBN 1 870754 64 6

Typesetting and reproduction by Viners Wood Associates. Printed in England by goodmanbaylis.

Below: Steam in the Sussex landscape! The Bluebell passes through some delightful Wealden scenery, which is exemplified in this view of No.473 *Birch Grove*, assisted in the rear by No.9017, pulling away from Freshfield Halt with a train bound for Sheffield Park on a sunny day in May 1963. The halt at Freshfield (which is concealed by the train) was the last survivor of the early Bluebell's three halts and, ironically, it was by far the smallest. Most Bluebell locomotives face northwards, but No.473 was an exception and was justly popular with photographers because of the opportunities it created. *David Clark*

Introduction

The history of the Lewes to East Grinstead line (part of which later became the Bluebell Railway) has been well documented over the years, but for the benefit of readers who may not be entirely familiar with the story I have compiled a very brief resume of past events which will, I hope, 'set the scene' and enhance your enjoyment of the photographs that follow. The first dozen or so pictures, which are of considerable historical interest, were taken during the final years of BR jurisdiction when the line was in its death throes and, I trust, convey some of the atmosphere of the route at that melancholy time.

The first, tentative steps towards the construction of the Lewes to East Grinstead Railway (LEGR) were taken on 30th September 1876 when a meeting of local gentry and landowners took place in Lewes. The area between the London, Brighton & South Coast Railway's (LBSCR) Brighton Line and the South Eastern Railway's Hastings Line had been a veritable battleground for many years and the latter company, supported by the London, Chatham & Dover Railway, had proposed various routes from London in order to compete for the lucrative traffic to Brighton. The LEGR failed to attract sufficient financial backing, however, and it became clear that it would never achieve its objective without substantial outside assistance. In 1878 a meeting took place between the LEGR and LBSCR and two directors of the latter company appeared on the board of the LEGR which gradually faded from the scene. The line between Lewes and East Grinstead opened on 1st August 1882, while the branch from Horsted Keynes to Haywards Heath opened for business on 3rd September of the following year.

The passenger service in the early years of the Lewes to East Grinstead line consisted of a mere six trains per day and goods traffic was of far greater importance. Most stations were provided with fair-sized goods yards which handled large consignments of timber, while substantial quantities of milk, usually destined for London, were also carried. In addition, farmers depended upon the line for the conveyance of livestock, grain and hay. For many years the line enjoyed considerable prosperity, but in the 1920s local dairies started to turn to motor transport and its monopoly of transport in the area began to be undermined. When the Southern Railway took over in 1923 receipts were in decline, a situation that was undoubtedly exacerbated by competition from motorbuses which eroded passenger income. In 1926 the 'Southern' made the first of a series of economies in which stations were grouped together under one stationmaster and some stations lost their signal boxes, platform buildings and footbridges. Meanwhile passenger services, which were powered by a variety of pre-grouping locomotive types, had increased to around a dozen trains (including short workings) every weekday south of Horsted Keynes.

When British Railways took over after the Second World War they were faced with a steadily increasing annual deficit which was causing much public criticism and BR sought to identify those routes which were losing money. In 1954 the British Transport Commission stated that the line made an annual loss of £59,000 and made the first moves towards closing the line. It was around this time that the route started to be known as the 'Bluebell Line'. Closure was eventually fixed for 13th June 1955, but in the event a footplatemen's strike meant that the last trains actually ran on 28th May. Much to BR's embarrassment, however, a local resident discovered that closure contravened the original Act of Parliament authorising the railway and on 7th August 1956 BR was forced to re-introduce services. These extraordinary and unprecedented events sparked a massive upsurge of public interest and were widely reported in the media. Despite the valiant efforts of local people to keep their line open, BR eventually prevailed and final closure took place on 16th March 1958, when large crowds witnessed the last train leave East Grinstead. The section south of Horsted Keynes closed completely, whilst the route north of there was retained on a 'care and maintenance' basis.

The first, hesitant moves to preserve the line were taken by three students who called a meeting in Haywards Heath on 15th March 1959 to form the Lewes-East Grinstead Railway Preservation Society, the name of which was changed to the Bluebell R.P.S. at a subsequent meeting on 14th June. The society sponsored a special train on 12th July which ran down the northern stretch of the line above Horsted Keynes and considerably helped to raise the society's profile. During the summer months members worked extremely hard on various tasks, including the repainting of Sheffield Park station, the clearance of vegetation and overhaul of signalling equipment. During the autumn delicate negotiations with BR continued and on Christmas Eve 1959 the society was offered a five years-long lease on the Sheffield Park to Horsted Keynes section totalling £2,250 per year. For Bluebell members it was the best Christmas present imaginable!

The first key event of 1960 was a packed public meeting at the Royal Pavilion, Brighton, on 19th February at which it was announced that the five-year lease had been accepted. A limited company, largely controlled by the society, had to be formed and a Light Railway Order obtained, the latter requiring notices in the press and a statutory time for any objections. After these legal procedures had been completed an exacting inspection took place on 9th July in order to satisfy the Ministry of Transport that the Bluebell Railway was competent to operate the railway and the final order was granted on 27th July. There were scenes of great joy at Sheffield Park station when the railway opened to the public on 7th August 1960.

I would like to thank all of the photographers who kindly offered material for this album, in particular R.C. Riley, who provided the bulk of the images from the very early days of the Bluebell. In addition, Chris Evans, David J. Fakes, Graham Mallinson and Roger Williams have scrutinised the manuscript and made many amendments and improvements to the text, although I accept responsibility for any errors that remain.

M. S. W., Burgess Hill, West Sussex, March 2005

One of the first, perhaps *the* first, colour photograph taken on the Lewes to East Grinstead line is this picture of Horsted Keynes station which is seen from the signal box steps on 30th April 1955. Judging by the newly repainted signs in the foreground, and scaffolding around the station house, the premises were undergoing renovation. A very generous layout was provided at Horsted Keynes, which was out of all proportion to the extremely modest amount of traffic on offer. In 1913 the LBSCR changed the track layout resulting in the downgrading of the westernmost platform, which had its buildings removed, and the reduction in status of the north signal box to a shunting frame. Further alterations took place in 1935 when electric trains were introduced on the Ardingly branch and Platform 1 (now designated Platform 2) became bi-directional, electric trains using a new crossover south of the signal box. This revised layout survived the early period of Bluebell operation prior to the purchase of the entire site in 1968, the diamond crossings eventually being taken out in the early 1970s. *R.C.Riley*

Another picture taken at Horsted Keynes station on 30th April 1955, this time looking southwards, and showing LBSCR K Class 'Mogul' No.32343 waiting in Platform 1 with the 3.28pm Haywards Heath to London Bridge train. This working, which later formed a down business train, was regularly comprised of seven coaches at this time, perhaps the heaviest passenger train of the day on the line north of Horsted Keynes. On this occasion it is made up of a SECR 'Birdcage' set, a Maunsell 3-set in carmine and cream livery, and an unidentified loose Maunsell vehicle on the rear. Note the rake of carriage underframes in the siding. The remarkably tall up starting signal, on the left, survives as Horsted Keynes' down advance starting signal. Preservation of a K Class LBSCR 'Mogul' was considered by the Bluebell, but at the time of their withdrawal the railway was using small locomotives almost exclusively and the K Class locomotives were reckoned to be too large for the line. Sadly, all of these engines went for scrap, which was a real tragedy because at least three of them had general overhauls not long before they were withdrawn. Today, a K Class locomotive would be considered ideal for the Bluebell! *R.C.Riley*

Curiously, despite its short length the Lewes to East Grinstead line boasted an exceptional mix of station designs, varying from the unusual 'double decker' station at East Grinstead to the single platform archetypal country station at Barcombe. Newick & Chailey was another unique station that was quite different to others on the line. It was built in a cutting just south of the main Haywards Heath to Uckfield road and because of the difficult location the main building was constructed on three levels. The basement was at platform level with the middle floor facing the forecourt, and the living quarters on the top floor. The enclosed flight of stairs down from the booking hall to platform level is clearly visible in this portrait which was taken in the mid-1950s. The station was also noteworthy because at one time a morning train to Lewes for schoolchildren started from there, returning in the afternoon. Surprisingly, the station building incorporated a refreshment room, the only one between Horsted Keynes and Lewes, and this drew most of its customers from much of the surrounding area, the patronage from rail travellers being negligible. Its closure in 1913 probably had more effect on the local populace than the closure of the station itself more than forty years later! Following closure the buildings survived for some years, but became increasingly dilapidated and were eventually demolished in 1967, a housing estate being built on the site. *R.C.Riley*

East Grinstead station was certainly not the largest in Sussex, but in many ways it was the most interesting because, in effect, it was two separate stations with the High Level platforms passing over the Low Level platforms at right angles, a most unusual arrangement. In this vintage illustration, taken on 7th May 1955, BR Standard Class 4 2-6-4T No.80033 poses at East Grinstead Low Level's down platform with a Victoria to Brighton train. One of the High Level station's platform canopies is visible above the locomotive. *Neil Davenport*

Puffy clouds scudding across the sky, trees just coming into leaf and the porter ambling up the platform ramp after exchanging the train staffs with the fireman of an unidentified Fairburn Class 4 2-6-4T waiting in the up platform. One can almost hear the birdsong and smell the fresh country air in this photographic masterpiece which beautifully captures the relaxed atmosphere of Sheffield Park station in the 1950s. Sadly, by the date of this picture, 7th May 1955, the death sentence for the Lewes to East Grinstead line had already been pronounced and such tranquil scenes were soon to pass into history. *Neil Davenport*

A further view of Sheffield Park station on 7th May 1955, looking northwards, with both platforms occupied by trains apparently formed of SECR 'Birdcage' sets of coaches. One cannot fail to notice the extremely shabby condition of the station's paintwork, which had obviously not been touched for many years. Note also the oil lamps, the fire buckets prominently 'displayed' and the premises' generally neat and tidy appearance. Incredibly, when the station was built two signal boxes were originally provided here, but in the mid-1930s they were replaced by an open signal frame on the down platform. Unfortunately this is largely concealed by the very deep shadows in this shot. When the Bluebell took over the hapless signalman became a target for intrigued children who were attracted by the bells and levers, and it was considered that an open signal frame compromised safety. A decision was made to enclose the frame and this work was undertaken during the winter of 1961/2. *Neil Davenport*

Left, above: The Railway Correspondence & Travel Society organised a 'last day' rail tour over the Lewes to East Grinstead line for 12th June 1955, but this was postponed due to a national strike by footplatemen. The train eventually ran on 14th August (more than two months after the official closure!), hauled by LBSCR 'Atlantic' No.32426 *St. Alban's Head*, which is seen here during a photographic stop at Horsted Keynes. It is possible that it was also taking water as well, but when the line was fully operational Sheffield Park was always the preferred spot to take water due to its much better supply. By this time, however, the line through Sheffield Park had been officially closed, so perhaps the water columns there had been taken out of use. *Colour-Rail*

Left, below: It must be admitted that this illustration has been published before, but the author considers this shot to be a real gem of a picture of great historical importance. It is one of the very few known colour photographs of a 'sulky service' train, which ran from 7th August 1956 until the line's final closure. These trains were provided by BR under duress following the discovery by a local resident that the original closure contravened the Act of Parliament authorising the railway: this required four trains to run stopping at certain stations. These 'sulky service' workings amounted to four trains a day, as stipulated in the original Act, but they ran without reference to other services and for a relatively short period in the middle of the day. These quite unprecedented developments caught the imagination of railway aficionados and the general public, many of whom took a 'fun' ride on the line they thought had gone forever. BR Standard Class 4 2-6-4T No.80154, pulling a single coach, leaves Horsted Keynes bound for East Grinstead on an unknown date in 1957. No.80154, the last locomotive built at Brighton Works, hauled some services over the line on its last day of operation. *Neil Sprinks*

The 11.30am Lewes to East Grinstead train pauses at West Hoathly station on 13th March 1958, just a few days before regular passenger services were withdrawn. LBSCR C2X Class locomotive No.32440 is in charge, probably hauling a single coach. This machine was one of 45 Billinton-designed C2 class engines that were rebuilt by Marsh with a larger boiler from 1908. The C2s, built by Vulcan Foundry, Newton-le-Willows, Lancashire, were always known to enginemen as 'Vulcans', so consequently the C2X class locomotives were referred to as 'Large Vulcans'. Unfortunately, the machine depicted here was one of the first of its class to be withdrawn, seven months after this picture was taken. A peculiar feature of this class was the double-domed boiler fitted to some engines. The second 'dome' on the boiler originally housed a top feed arrangement which was later removed, although the 'dome' was left in position on the boiler top. The final survivors of this class were withdrawn in 1962 and, regrettably, no examples were retained for preservation. *R. C. Riley*

Another view of East Grinstead's 'double decker' station. The first line to reach East Grinstead was the branch from Three Bridges, which opened on 9th July 1855: this link was extended to Tunbridge Wells in October 1866. In 1882 the route southwards to Lewes opened whilst the line from Oxted opened for business in March 1884. The tracks in the foreground are those from Lewes to Oxted (and London), while the High Level was largely served by trains between Three Bridges and Tunbridge Wells. The station's remarkable layout is clearly visible in this picture which was taken on 13th March 1958. In addition there was a tightly-curved connection between the west end of the High Level station and St. Margarets Junction, half a mile north of the Low Level station. There was also a goods spur between the High and Low Level yards. Regrettably, the impressive station building, on the right, was demolished by BR in the early 1970s. *R. C. Riley*

A 4 miles-long branch from Copyhold Junction, north of Haywards Heath, to Horsted Keynes was included in the original Lewes and East Grinstead Railway Bill of 1878. The idea was to provide direct connection between coastal towns in east Sussex and stations on the secondary route to London via East Grinstead. It was brought into use without ceremony on 3rd September 1883, over a year after the Lewes to East Grinstead line opened. The short branch was notable for two major engineering features, the 215 yards-long Lywood tunnel, and the five-arch Sherriff Mill viaduct just outside Horsted Keynes station. Unfortunately, the expectations of the line's promoters of housing development on the route were not fulfilled and the branch was always a sleepy backwater. The electrification of the line in 1935 failed to bring prosperity to the branch, which only came to life at the beginning and end of Ardingly College's school terms. This view shows Ardingly station on 17th May 1959: note that the main station building, which is partially visible on the right, is located on a higher level than the platforms and reached by an extension of the footbridge. In 1959 brand new Kent Coast electric stock was berthed on the down line between Ardingly and Horsted Keynes and when this entered service displaced locomotive-hauled vehicles were dumped there prior to scrapping. The site of Ardingly station is now occupied by a stone terminal.

R. C. Riley

LBSCR C2X Class 0-6-0 No.32535 pauses at Horsted Keynes with a rail tour on 12th July 1959. The train started from Tonbridge and ran via East Grinstead (where the goods only spur was used between the high and low level yards) to Horsted Keynes, and later returned to Tonbridge via Haywards Heath, Lewes and Uckfield. On arrival at Horsted Keynes the Bluebell chairman addressed the participants from a signal post.

Colour-Rail

Following official closure of the Lewes to East Grinstead line in March 1958, the route north of Horsted Keynes was not completely closed, but retained on a 'care and maintenance' basis. The up line was used for the storage of condemned freight wagons prior to scrapping, whilst the down line was available for special traffic purposes. Furthermore, the down line could also be used as an up line as required, in which case it was necessary to institute single-line working by pilotman between Horsted Keynes and East Grinstead. This method of working ceased after the passage of the final, and probably the only, up train on each occasion: unscheduled workings along the down line required no special arrangements. On 27th September 1959 a ramblers' special to Ardingly, hauled by 'Battle of Britain' Class No.34068 *Kenley*, traversed the line south of East Grinstead and is seen here at Horsted Keynes. The first coach immediately behind the locomotive conveyed members of the fledgling Bluebell Railway Preservation Society who were attending a rally day at Sheffield Park, where a pump trolley was in action in order to demonstrate the operation of recently installed signalling at that location. The down line to Ardingly was being used for storage of withdrawn stock at the time of this picture so, in order to resume its journey southwards, *Kenley* would have needed to propel its train out of the station in order to cross on to the up line. It would then have had to pass through Platform 1 (now known as Platform 2) in order to reach the former Ardingly branch up line. This track had been re-signalled for use as a bi-directional line while the former down line had, in effect, become a siding. Note the rather colourful collection of coaches in the siding on the left of the picture, all of which appear to be branded with the dreaded condemned sign, commonly known to railwaymen as a 'hot cross bun'. Many coaches, especially those rendered redundant by the Kent Coast electrification, were temporarily stored at Horsted Keynes before making their last journey to Newhaven for scrapping. So, at that time, if you were a railway enthusiast with a special interest in withdrawn coaches or wagons, the line between Horsted Keynes and East Grinstead really was something of a 'Mecca'! *Colour-Rail*

This illustration of Horsted Keynes was taken from an unusual position at the entrance to the goods yard, with the track into the yard in the foreground. A four-coach electric train to Seaford is pulling out from Platform 1 with an unidentified '2-Hal' unit leading. In addition to wagons in the yard, which do not often appear in pictures taken at Horsted Keynes, this photograph also depicts the water tank, on the left, in complete condition with its tank in place. The tracks on the immediate left are, of course, those to Lewes and they appear to have a thick covering of rust indicating that no trains had traversed the line since closure. Note the splendid cloud formation! *Colour-Rail*

It is commonly supposed that LBSCR 'Terrier' No.55 *Stepney* was the first steam locomotive to have arrived at Sheffield Park after the Bluebell's takeover but, in fact, the first arrival was the Narrow Gauge Railway Society's diminutive engine *Townsend Hook* which was temporarily stored in the goods yard. Following the successful conclusion of delicate negotiations with BR, the first really tangible sign of progress was the arrival at Sheffield Park of the Bluebell's first items of rolling stock. At approximately 4.45pm on 17th May 1960 No.55 *Stepney*, accompanied by the railway's first two coaches, steamed into Sheffield Park station to be greeted not only by an excited and enthusiastic group of society members but also press and television representatives. A two-hour filming session ensued for the benefit of the television crews. A second locomotive, SECR P Class No.323, followed on 27th June. This picture was taken on 3rd July 1960 during a trial run and depicts the entire rolling stock fleet owned by the Bluebell during its first season. *Stepney* is out of sight at the far end of the train. Note that one of the coaches has already been repainted in blue livery preparatory to opening to the public just over a month later. *R. C. Riley*

Left, above: Before the Bluebell Railway could carry members of the public it had to obtain a Light Railway Order, which involved a thorough inspection by Colonel J.R.H. Robertson, of the Ministry of Transport, to verify its fitness and competence to operate the line safely. The inspection took place on 9th July 1960 and the final order was granted on 27th July. It was decided to open to the public on 7th August, and prior to that date a huge 'behind the scenes' effort was made to ensure that everything ran smoothly. Tickets and timetables had to be printed, a bookstall set up for the sale of souvenirs and, most importantly, refreshments organised. Owing to limited accommodation a draw was held to decide which members would travel on the inaugural train. The opening ceremony took place on the running plate of SECR P Class locomotive No.323 *Bluebell* from which the society's chairman, John Leroy, introduced the guests of honour, Captain Anthony Kimmins, the well-known playright, and his wife, to a huge gathering of members and well-wishers. After a short speech by Captain Kimmins, cameras clicked as Mrs. Kimmins christened *Bluebell* in the traditional manner, the events being reported in the national media. In this shot Captain Kimmins is seen addressing the crowd from the front of *Bluebell* shortly before it set off, accompanied by *Stepney*, with the first, history-making, train to Horsted Keynes (Bluebell Halt).
John Millbank

Left, below: Another photograph taken on the Bluebell's first day of public operation, which appears to show the rear of an empty train reversing out of Sheffield Park station before crossing over on to the up line. *Bluebell* is at the front of the train with *Stepney*, complete with a tail lamp, on the rear. It is recorded that on the first day well over 2,000 people witnessed the opening ceremony and the railway carried more than 900 passengers. A special guest was Mrs. Sarah Funnell, aged ninety-two, a resident of Barcombe who witnessed the construction of the line. Luckily, the society was blessed with good weather, the sun apparently shining throughout the entire afternoon. *John Millbank*

A general view of the south end of Sheffield Park station on 28th August 1960, by which time the euphoria of the opening had died down and the society members were getting down to the routine business of running the railway on a regular basis. On the left of the picture the cattle dock is visible, together with parked cars in the goods yard. The building immediately to the right of the train is the uncompleted engine shed, whilst the pump house just edges into the shot on the extreme right. Perhaps the locomotive inspection pit was the most vital piece of infrastructure constructed by the Bluebell but this, of course, is not clearly visible. It is located in the pump house siding. *R. C. Riley*

Left, above: During the 1960/61 winter one of the major jobs was the repainting of No.55 *Stepney* which was, presumably, mostly undertaken in the open. Here we see No.55 more or less incognito, with large areas of undercoat visible on the side tanks and cab sides. Luckily the spring was mild and March 1961 was dry, thus enabling the team of painters to complete *Stepney*'s exquisite transformation from BR black to her former LBSCR colours in time for the Easter re-opening. This picture was taken at Sheffield Park on 11th March 1961.
R. C. Riley

Left, below: The acquisition of some of London Transport's historic rake of coaches from the Chesham branch, which dated from the turn of the century, had been one of the Bluebell's objectives for some time, and this aim was realised when the coaches were delivered on 2nd March 1961. In this picture coach No.518, formerly Metropolitan Railway No.394, is seen receiving attention to its roof canvas at Sheffield Park on 11th March, just over a week after its arrival. Interestingly, this coach operated for a time as part of an electric unit: note the driver's controls and large look-out windows which can be seen through the open cab door. It was reconverted for steam operation in about 1941. *R. C. Riley*

The 1961 season opened on 1st April and, apart from members in Victorian costume which became a regular feature of Bluebell events, the main attraction was the first public appearance of the newly-restored *Stepney* which looked resplendent in LBSCR livery. The Chesham coaches also made their first revenue-earning working on that day. Before the departure of the first train, the society's President, the Reverend Geoffrey H. Warde, Bishop of Lewes, formerly bestowed the name *Primrose* upon SECR P class locomotive No.27. In this picture the pair are depicted reversing out of the down platform at Sheffield Park before crossing over to the up line, with another train to Horsted Keynes. *R. C. Riley*

The first locomotive to arrive at Sheffield Park under the Bluebell's jurisdiction was, as previously mentioned, this diminutive 0-4-0T engine No.4 *Townsend Hook* which arrived on 8th April 1960. This 3ft. 2¼in. gauge locomotive was built by Fletcher Jennings & Co. of Whitehaven in 1880 and worked at the Dorking Greystone Lime Company's quarry at Betchworth until the installation closed in 1960. The engine was named after a former chairman of the company. It was owned by the Narrow Gauge Railway Society and is seen here standing on a short piece of track at Sheffield Park on 16th April 1961. The locomotive was later moved to a museum at Brockham in Surrey and, at the time of writing, can be seen at the Chalk Pits Museum, Amberley. *Neil Davenport*

In the distant days when the Bluebell Railway had a main line connection and BR steam traction was still in operation, the railway occasionally arranged rail tours, Bluebell Special No.2 taking place on 22nd April 1961. The special left Brighton for Horsham with, appropriately, two LBSCR locomotives in charge, E4 class No.32503 being the leading locomotive whilst E6 Class No.32418 was on the rear of the train. The latter had been in store at Brighton shed for some time prior to the trip and, unfortunately, sustained a hot axle box which necessitated its removal at Three Bridges. There another, totally unprepared, E4 Class engine, No.32564, was attached for the rest of day's proceedings. A run to East Grinstead was next on the itinerary and, following reversal, the train then continued to Oxted, where it reversed once again and headed for the 'Cuckoo' line. The highlight of the afternoon was undoubtedly a stirring climb up the 1 in 88 to Rotherfield. On arrival at Polegate, No.32503 was replaced, as planned, by sister engine No.32479 and the excursionists continued to Lewes and later reached Horsted Keynes. On arrival there most participants took a return trip to Sheffield Park, the heavy rain of earlier in the day having given way to brilliant evening sunshine. The special later returned to Brighton with the same E4 Class locomotives in charge, arrival being at around 8.30pm. In this picture a rather grimy No.32564 is seen waiting north of Horsted Keynes station before leaving for Brighton. This locomotive had given a good account of itself despite being commandeered at short notice. *R. C. Riley*

Preserved locomotives do not come much finer than the Adams 'Radial' tank, which is surely one of the most attractive, perhaps *the* most attractive, engine in the Bluebell's fleet. No.488 poses in the up platform at Sheffield Park station on 19th July 1961, exactly a week after its arrival on Bluebell metals. The class was introduced for the LSWR in 1882 and this particular example was built by Neilson & Co.'s Glasgow works in 1885. The class was used on suburban trains from Waterloo station, but as early as 1915 was being displaced by electric units and by the late 1920s only two representatives remained in service, on the Axminster to Lyme Regis branch in rural Devon. In the meantime No.488 had been sold to the government in 1916, which in turn sold it to the East Kent Railway in 1919, becoming their No.5. By 1946 age was beginning to take its toll of the other two 'Radial' tanks, both of which required extensive overhaul, but owing to the extremely tight curves on the Lyme Regis branch the Southern Railway's efforts to find suitable replacements were unsuccessful. So, No.488 was purchased to relieve the pressure on the other two veterans and continued to work the line until it was partially relaid in the early 1960s thus allowing the 'Radial' locomotives to be withdrawn. Purchase of an example of this graceful design had been one of the society's objectives from the very early days and this was realised when No.488 arrived from Eastleigh on 12th July 1961.

R.C. Riley

Right, above: During the Bluebell's first season, and for nearly all of the 1961 season, trains were not permitted to enter Horsted Keynes BR station and were obliged to terminate at Horsted Keynes (Bluebell Halt), a newly constructed station on the other side of the road bridge to the main station. This station, which had been built entirely by Bluebell volunteers, was merely a wooden platform without any kind of shelter: it was approached by means of a footpath from the road. Owing to the lack of a run-round loop Bluebell Railway trains were worked by two engines, one at each end of the train, so this unusual method of operation, which may have been a nuisance for the Bluebell, was at least of interest to the railway enthusiast fraternity. In order to provide a modicum of shelter for potential travellers at the halt, and also a booking office facility, a coach was usually berthed at the north end of the platform. In this picture a train headed by *Primrose* is seen arriving at Horsted Keynes on 20th August 1961.

Trevor Owen

Right, below: Another view of the train seen in the previous shot, showing *Bluebell* at the other end of the formation waiting to leave Horsted Keynes (Bluebell Halt) for Sheffield Park. When Bluebell trains were permitted to run into Horsted Keynes BR station the halt was rendered redundant and was later closed. It remained intact for some years in a deteriorating condition and was later removed, and no trace of the structure now remains.

Trevor Owen

On a sunny 17th September 1961 locomotive Nos. 55 *Stepney* and 488, the Adams 'Radial' tank, wait at the south end of Sheffield Park station whilst the former takes water. When this vital operation had been completed they would have shunted the empty stock across to the up line to form another train to Horsted Keynes. Note the group of admirers standing on the platform. By the date of this photograph No.488 had been a resident at Sheffield Park for more than two months and its blistered BR paintwork had clearly benefited from the lavish attention of the engine cleaners: certainly it is in sparkling condition in this shot. Pictures of this machine working on the Bluebell in BR black livery during the period covered by this book are hard to find because it was repainted into LSWR livery during the following winter. Unfortunately, at the time of writing No.488 is out of service awaiting overhaul, work which may necessitate provision of a replacement boiler. *R. C. Riley*

Right: An illustration of the layout immediately north of Horsted Keynes station on 29th October 1961. This picture also gives a good view of the extremely tall LBSCR up starting signal at this location. Note the instruction to enginemen on the water crane. Water pressure was notoriously low at Horsted Keynes, doubtless due to the station's elevation, and in BR days locomotives usually took water at Sheffield Park which had a much better supply. Note the red flag and sleeper across the rails indicating the limit of Bluebell operations. *John Beckett*

In the early days of the Bluebell Railway on special occasions staff used to dress in period costume and in this picture, taken in about 1961, a cheerful group of ladies make a colourful sight at Horsted Keynes. The crew of *Stepney*, which is partially visible, has evidently been persuaded to join them. The Bluebell tradition of wearing Victorian dress at special events, which was very popular with the general public, seems to have faded over the years. Perhaps it should be revived! *Tom Martin collection*

The year 1961 was a momentous one for the Bluebell Railway in many ways, the several notable achievements including the restoration of *Stepney*, acquisition of the Adams 'Radial' tank locomotive and the highly successful experimental period of sixteen days continuous running in August during which 15,000 passengers were carried. It is interesting to record that, in those days, trains ran much later in the day and during August 1961 there was a departure at 6.30pm from Sheffield Park. The culmination of the season came on the very last day, 29th October, when the Bluebell made history by running into Horsted Keynes station, the first time a privately preserved railway had operated on BR tracks. *Stepney* and the Adams 'Radial' No.488 headed the train, with the two P Class locomotives on the rear. In this superb panoramic view of Horsted Keynes station, seen on the first day of through operation, the diminutive P Class engines can just be discerned. This shot was taken from the top of the water tank, which has long since been removed, so this photograph cannot be repeated. *R. C. Riley*

Photographed in absolutely stunning late afternoon autumn sunshine, *Bluebell* and *Primrose* make an energetic departure from Horsted Keynes on 29th October 1961 with *Stepney* and the Adams 'Radial' tank locomotive No.488 bringing up the rear. The train appears to be crammed with passengers, all no doubt determined to ride on the first, history-making Bluebell working from Horsted Keynes. One wonders what the gentleman in the foreground, who is standing quite close to a live rail, is trying to achieve!

John Beckett

On 15th February 1962 Great Western Railway 'Dukedog' locomotive No.9017 arrived at Sheffield Park, by far the largest engine in the Bluebell's fleet at that time. The locomotive had been purchased by a private preservation fund and was offered 'on loan' to the Bluebell Railway, where it has been based ever since. No.9017 was the last surviving standard gauge locomotive on BR with outside frames, ending its days at Aberystwyth shed on the former Cambrian Railway system in Wales. One of its last recorded duties was powering the 11.5am train from Dovey Junction to Pwllheli on 30th September 1960. Following withdrawal in October 1960, No.9017 was stored in the old Cambrian Railway works at Oswestry whilst funds were raised for its preservation. The locomotive arrived at Sheffield Park under its own steam, having visited Brighton shed for turning purposes before proceeding to the Bluebell. In this illustration it is depicted shunting at Sheffield Park on 25th March 1962 and is in BR condition, complete with front number plate and totem on the tender. *Roy Hobbs*

Left, above: The year 1962 saw the first full season of Bluebell operation into Horsted Keynes station thus linking up with BR for the first time. An additional sign was attached to the running-in board in the background inviting passengers to 'Alight Here For The Bluebell Line'. The Bluebell management probably hoped that this interchange facility would stimulate traffic on the little-used Haywards Heath to Horsted Keynes branch and save it from oblivion. Alas, it was not to be! The branch was closed by BR on 27th October 1963 which was, by a most regrettable coincidence, almost exactly two years to the day after the Bluebell's historic first train ran into Horsted Keynes station. In this picture No.323 *Bluebell* is seen departing southwards on 1st April 1962. *Bruce Jenkins*

Left, below: The 'Chesham' set of coaches which was used very intensively in the early 1960s, is seen here at Sheffield Park on 1st April 1962 following repainting. These vehicles were originally built at the turn of the century for the Metropolitan Railway. The set was later converted (as previously mentioned) for electric operation which included modifying the outermost compartments of some vehicles as driving cabs, complete with driver's controls and large end look-out windows. The coach nearest to the camera in this picture has been modified in this way. During the Second World War the set was reconverted for steam working and was based on the Chesham branch until electrification in 1960. The set is currently undergoing painstaking restoration and three vehicles have already been returned to service.

Colour-Rail

In the early 1960s there were few privately preserved locomotives, one of this select band being Great Northern Railway (GNR) 0-6-0ST No.1247, which was the very first engine to be bought for private operational preservation. No.1247's owner enjoyed very cordial relations with the Bluebell Railway, and the 'Blue Belle' rail tour with the locomotive as motive power was arranged for 1st April 1962. The train started from London Bridge station, No.1247 having spent the night at Bricklayers Arms shed after travelling from its base at Hatfield the previous evening. The train reached Haywards Heath without incident, where it reversed before running to Horsted Keynes, *Stepney* then taking over at the head of the train for the run to Sheffield Park with No.1247 on the rear. In this scene, recorded at Sheffield Park, No.1247 is standing on the right, whilst *Bluebell* waits at the head of the Chesham set of coaches. *R. C. Riley*

Left: The Bluebell's guest of honour on the occasion of the 'Blue Belle' rail tour was the late Doctor Richard (later Lord) Beeching, chairman of the British Transport Commission. The decision to invite Doctor Beeching was controversial and did not meet with the wholehearted approval of Bluebell members, bearing in mind his role in the cutbacks of the BR system. During a short ceremony he officially opened a new halt at Holywell (Waterworks) and, apparently, later gave the preservation movement his blessing. He is seen here with a Bluebell driver at Sheffield Park. *John Millbank*

A general view of the south end of Sheffield Park station on 1st April 1962, with the GNR saddle tank locomotive waiting to leave at the rear of the 'Blue Belle' special train returning to London. This photograph also shows the erstwhile cattle dock siding with its associated pens which were a feature of many rural wayside stations. Prior to the train's departure Doctor Beeching inspected the newly-constructed signal box on the down platform. Another guest was Mr. George Weeden, Line Traffic Manager of the Southern Region's Central Section, without whose enthusiastic co-operation the special train would not have run. *R. C. Riley*

Some of the Bluebell Railway's famous collection of vintage enamel advertisements are seen here in this series of photographs. These pictures were all taken in the early 1960s. *John Edgington*

TURNERS of LEWES
DRY OAK FOR JOINERY
ALL TYPES OF FENCING
SUPPLIED AND FIXED
Head Office: 35 HIGH STREET, LEWES. Tel. 2252
THIS SAWMILL WAS FIRST
ESTABLISHED AT NUTLEY IN 1830
AND MOVED HERE IN 1896 TO HAVE
ITS OWN RAILWAY SIDINGS
COLMAN'S MUSTARD
VOLVOLUTUM The World's Best SOAP
Daily Telegraph
BRASSO
Waverley Pen
WILLS'S GOLD FLAKE CIGARETTES 10-3
SOLD HERE "OLD FRIEND" TOBACCO
WRIGHT'S COALTAR SOAP
SPRATT'S OVALS
GINGER NUTS
COLMAN'S MUSTARD
LUBRICANTS
RAILWAY
Castrol
JAMES DOME BLACK LEAD
ROYAL HOUSEHOLD

OGDEN'S
"GUINEA-GOLD"
CIGARETTES.
3d Per Packet of 10, BEWARE OF IMITATIONS.
WILLS'S
GOLD FLAKE
CIGARETTES
W.D.&H.O.WILLS
CIGARETTES SOLD HERE.
"WILD WOODBINE"
WILD WOODBINE
CIGARETTES
W.D.&H.O.WILLS
BRISTOL & LONDON
CIGARETTES
FRY'S
HOCOLATE
CHURCHMAN'S
"TORTOISESHELL"
SMOKING MIXTURE.
WILLS'S
Rich Cut Virginia
TOBACCO
4½D an Ounce
VOLVOLUT
NO RUBBING! NO SOAKING!!
MRS 'V' SOAP

Left: A general view of the crowds at Sheffield Park station on 1st April 1962. Due to the large number of people waiting on the platform, the fireman of No.323 *Bluebell* is clearly unable to see what is happening at the other end of the train! It is doubtful whether the Bluebell would normally be quite so busy at this time of year, and it is likely that most of these folk (predominantly gentlemen!) were railway enthusiasts who had travelled down from London on the special.

Neil Davenport

The visit of GNR No.1247 attracted huge crowds to the Bluebell and in this picture the returning special train is seen passing Holywell (Waterworks) Halt, which is hidden by the train, and approaching a group of onlookers standing in a field adjacent to the line. The train is headed by the Adams 'Radial' tank locomotive No.488, whilst the GNR engine is on the rear. Judging by the amount of cloud in the sky the photographer appears to have been lucky with sun! On the return journey to London No.1247 performed brilliantly and was routed via the Quarry Line, while the 'Brighton Belle' was reportedly relegated to the slower route via Redhill! *Trevor Owen*

By virtue of being one of the earliest standard gauge preserved railways, the Bluebell Railway was in the fortunate position of being able to acquire historic locomotives and coaches straight out of BR service, and has never had to resort to industrial engines. Two of the very few industrial locomotives seen at Sheffield Park are pictured here, in this shot taken on 8th July 1962. The tiny engine nearest to the camera is No.25, which was previously employed by the North Thames Gas Board at Beckton gasworks. This little engine, which was built to a restricted loading gauge for use in the retort houses, arrived at the Bluebell on 25th October 1961, on loan from the Industrial Railway Society. The other machine is *Baxter*, an 0-4-0T locomotive built by Fletcher Jennings of Whitehaven, Cumberland, in 1877. It worked at Betchworth quarry, between Dorking and Reigate, for many years and was unnamed and unnumbered until the 1920s, when it became No.3 *Captain Baxter.* In 1947 it was renamed *Baxter* and a nameplate was fitted. The locomotive finished work in 1959 and arrived at the Bluebell on 15th August 1960. It had a brief sortie on a passenger train at the end of the 1960 season, which at least proved its unsuitability for such work(!), but *Baxter* is a particularly appealing little engine and is useful for light shunting duties and pilot work.

Alan Chandler

On 21st October 1962 the Bluebell ran another rail tour, this time from Victoria to Sheffield Park. The train was named the 'Victory Belle' and employed preserved LSWR T9 Class 4-4-0 No.120 on the main line sections to and from Haywards Heath. Bluebell engines worked the train between Haywards Heath and Sheffield Park, the motive power between Haywards Heath and Horsted Keynes being *Stepney* and the 'Adams' Radial tank locomotive, whilst the newly arrived LBSCR E4 Class 0-6-2T No.473 (formerly BR No.32473) officiated to and from Sheffield Park. Here, the latter locomotive poses after arrival with the 'Victory Belle' and appears to be attracting a large group of admirers on possibly its first public appearance following its arrival at the Bluebell in full working order only five days previously. The E4 Class locomotive was undoubtedly a welcome addition to the Bluebell's historic collection of vintage motive power. It should be noted that, at this time, 'The Blue Belle' headboard was carried on rail tours sponsored by the Bluebell Railway apparently regardless of the train's official title! *Tom Martin collection*

A further illustration of No.473, taken on the same day as the previous picture, showing it working the 'Wealden Rambler', *en route* for Sheffield Park, near Holywell (Waterworks) Halt. The first two digits of its former BR running number and totem on the tankside have been painted over. This class originally consisted of 75 examples, but by the time of this picture only a handful remained in BR use, so the purchase of this engine was timely. This particular locomotive was built in 1898 at Brighton Works and is notable for two forays it made onto BR metals before removal of the track between Ardingly and Horsted Keynes. *R. C. Riley*

A number of Bluebell members considered that a halt should be built at Holywell (Waterworks) because of its location on the Haywards Heath to Horsted Keynes bus route. The structure, which was by far the best equipped of the railway's halts, boasted a small covered waiting area and even a tiny ticket office: no expense was spared. It opened in April 1962, but became an immediate headache for the Bluebell because most passengers arrived by car, their parked vehicles causing congestion on the adjacent narrow country road. This prompted complaints from the local authority which wanted the entrance moved to a safer location. The number of customers was minimal, only fifty tickets apparently being booked there during the entire 1962 season, and with the continued opposition of the authorities the Bluebell had little choice but to close the halt at the end of the season. The building was removed during the 1963/64 close season, the materials being use elsewhere on the line. Here, *Primrose* is seen on (what appears to be) a Sheffield Park-bound train, also on 21st October 1962. *John Beckett*

Left, above: Another shot of the 'Victory Belle' rail tour, this time showing the train ambling along the Ardingly branch on the second stage of its journey back to the capital. The two vintage locomotives hauling the train hardly need an introduction! The train looks most strange running over the former up line, which was converted for bi-directional running when the former down line between Ardingly and Horsted Keynes was made into a siding on 16th January 1959 to facilitate the storage of new Kent Coast electric stock. The signal, therefore, was a recent installation dating from the time of the change of use of the tracks. *Colour-Rail*

Left, below: When the Bluebell Railway took over the line there was no covered accommodation whatsoever available for rolling stock and the erection of an engine shed was top priority. For the first few years of the line's existence the building seen here in November 1962 was the only accommodation available to protect the railway's priceless collection of veteran locomotives. It was just as well the Bluebell's fleet consisted mainly of small engines! *Roy Hobbs*

Right, above: The start of the 1963 season was marked by the successful running of the 'Spring Belle' rail tour from London Victoria to Sheffield Park and return on 31st March. On this occasion the Bluebell was given permission to use LBSCR No.473 *Birch Grove* as motive power on the down run, assisted by BR Standard 2-6-4T No.80084. Sister engine No.80154 had been requested, but it was unavailable. A top speed of 64mph was attained at Three Bridges and when the train reached Haywards Heath the BR Standard tank locomotive proceeded to Brighton for servicing whilst No.473 and the Adams 'Radial' tank engine took the train on to the Bluebell Railway. On arrival at Sheffield Park the principal event was the naming of *Birch Grove* which had been restored to Marsh umber livery during the winter. On the return trip from Haywards Heath to London, with No.80084 this time in sole charge, the journey from Haywards Heath to Victoria was accomplished in 47 minutes and at one point the train was running four minutes early. Here, the rear of the returning special (hauled by the Adams locomotive) is seen at Holywell (Waterworks) Halt with No.473 assisting at the back, followed by coach No.971 and *Bluebell*. The reason for this unusual formation is unclear, but presumably No.971 was forming an ordinary timetabled Bluebell train for which a separate pathway was not available. *Alan Chandler*

Left, below: On most preserved railways steam locomotives have the highest profile and are in the limelight much more than are carriages, but during the first half of 1963 developments with the Bluebell's carriage fleet were noteworthy. The 24th of February saw the arrival of the LNWR observation car, which was built in 1913. It had latterly been employed on scenic routes in north Wales, but was displaced by diesel units in 1958. It later became the only surviving pre-grouping observation car and the sole standard gauge example of a double-ended car in regular operation. The car, seen here in May 1963, is very popular with the passengers and has probably travelled more miles in Bluebell service than any other item of rolling stock. *R.C. Riley*

Soon after the Bluebell opened it quickly became famous as a home for beautifully restored locomotives and vintage carriages. For many people the highlight of a visit was, of course, the chance to travel in an ancient carriage, so some visitors in May 1963 may have been disappointed to find their train composed of relatively modern coaches, identical to those found in large numbers at that time on the BR system. This was explained by the fact that London Transport had requested the loan of the 'Chesham' set of Metropolitan Railway coaches for an event at Neasden depot commemorating the opening of the world's first underground railway. This was opened by the Metropolitan Railway between Paddington Bishop's Road and Farringdon Street on 10th January 1863. While the set was away BR loaned six carriages so the Bluebell was not short of stock. In this picture, taken on 26th May 1963, *Birch Grove* stands at the rear of a train formed of some of the BR stock, which consisted of a mixture of BR Standard and Bulleid carriages. The coach nearest to the camera is a BR Standard Mk.I vehicle whilst the next two are Bulleid-designed coaches. *Neil Davenport*

How many times have the words 'a never to be forgotten occasion' been uttered in relation to the Bluebell? One such memorable event was the visit of the beautiful Caledonian Railway 'Single' No.123 on the 'Scottish Belle' rail tour on 15th September 1963. The special started in London, the train engine for both legs of the main line run being T9 Class No.120, with No.123 as pilot, and the former certainly performed well on the journey down from Victoria to Haywards Heath. The veteran 'Single' was, understandably perhaps, soon out of breath on the climbs and arrived at Haywards Heath decidedly low on steam pressure. The train was taken over there by Adams 'Radial' No.488 piloting *Birch Grove* and the pair are seen approaching Ardingly. *Colour-Rail*

After the arrival of the 'Scottish Belle' at Haywards Heath CR No.123 and the T9 went down to Brighton shed to be turned, coaled and watered. When those tasks had been completed they ran up to Horsted Keynes in the afternoon and are seen here approaching Ardingly station. The train was officially named the 'Scottish Belle', but confusingly, it carried a headboard with the title 'The Blue Belle'. No.123 was built by Neilson & Co. of Glasgow in 1886 and ran in service until 1935 when it was set aside for static preservation. In 1958 the Scottish Region made the inspired decision to restore the locomotive to full working order for use on rail tours, although a trip to Sussex was probably not what they had in mind! *John Beckett*

The Caledonian Railway 'Single' No.123 and T9 Class No.120 pose for photographers at Horsted Keynes after their arrival from Brighton. Unfortunately, the engines were facing north, which made photography tricky, and it had been hoped that the two machines could go on display in the goods yard, but this was not possible. Despite the difficulties the immaculate pair of veterans drew an unprecedented crowd of around 2,000 people to Horsted Keynes, part of the gathering being visible on the extreme right of the shot. The 'Scottish Belle' went back to Haywards Heath with the same locomotives that had performed earlier and the train returned to Victoria with a contented complement of passengers, a top speed of 68mph being recorded on two occasions. The 'Single' returned to Willesden shed later the same evening on the first stage of its long journey home to Scotland. *Greg Child, John Edgington collection*

A Horsted Keynes to Seaford train, formed of '2 Bil' unit No.2034, leaves Ardingly station. This is another picture that was taken on 15th September 1963, a day on which every railway enthusiast in the south of England appears to have descended on the Bluebell Railway and the Ardingly branch. The glorious weather doubtless encouraged photography! One reason often advanced for electrification of this branch was the operating convenience of running trains through to Horsted Keynes to reverse, rather than reversing at Haywards Heath station. The latter is a particularly busy station and the operating authorities would have wished to avoid unnecessary conflicting movements with trains on the Brighton Line. *Colour-Rail*

The year 1964 was not the happiest on the Bluebell Railway. Following the closure of the Ardingly branch during the previous autumn the Bluebell had become isolated from the BR system and in July demolition contractors started their 'lethal work' (as it was described in the society's journal at the time) lifting the line west and north of Horsted Keynes. Furthermore, the Bluebell's five-year lease was running out and this doubtless loomed large in the minds of many members. BR had indicated that a renewal would not be permitted, so the Bluebell would have to find an enormous sum to purchase the line. Clearly fund raising was a vital issue, the success or failure of which would determine the future of the whole Bluebell enterprise. But 1964 was not quite all doom and gloom! One of the railway's P Class tank locomotives, No.27 *Primrose*, had been restored to full SECR green passenger livery and in this view, taken in the spring of that year at Horsted Keynes, it is a joy to behold. Could there have been a more attractive and elaborate colour scheme? *David Clark*

The Blue Circle was photographed at Sheffield Park in May 1964, shortly after its delivery to the Bluebell. This mechanical curiosity was built in 1926 by Aveling & Porter Ltd. of Rochester, Kent, for use at the Snodland works of the Holborough Cement Company. The former firm was noted for its more numerous road locomotives and rollers and this engine was clearly based on these traditional designs. In 1931 the Snodland works was taken over by Associated Portland Cement Manufacturers who continued to find employment for *The Blue Circle* until it was pensioned off in 1963. It was presented to the Bluebell Railway in 1964 and steamed on a number of occasions for brake van trips. It left the Bluebell some years ago and is now to be seen at the Buckinghamshire Railway Centre, Quainton Road. *Roy Hobbs*

The Hayling Island branch, which had a severe weight restriction, had been the last sanctuary for the LBSCR 'Terriers' and following the withdrawal of services the opportunity arose for the Bluebell to purchase a further locomotive of that class. The Bluebell selected No.32636, formerly LBSCR No.72 *Fenchurch*, which at the time of its withdrawal had attained the stately age of 91 years and was the oldest locomotive in BR service. The engine arrived on the Bluebell on 13th May 1964 accompanied by a LBSCR milk van that had been bought by a group of members. They had the distinction of being the last stock to arrive via the moribund Ardingly branch before track lifting commenced, the van being propelled by No.32636 without a brake van, a most unorthodox example of railway operating for which special permission was obtained. The Bluebell quickly renumbered their latest addition 2636 which is depicted leaving Horsted Keynes with a southbound train on 30th May 1964. The Southdown-liveried bus visible in the background was owned by a Bluebell member and was not operating a scheduled service. *R. C. Riley*

Left: An everyday scene at the south end of Sheffield Park station, showing *Bluebell* imaginatively framed by the platform canopy, while a group of members, on the right, appear to be in deep conversation. This picture was taken on 12th September 1964. This proved to be No.323's last full year in service in black livery, because it was taken out of traffic for repair in mid-1965. It was ceremoniously returned to service on 4th September 1966 fully repainted in the railway's own livery of 'Bluebell blue', lined with light blue, black, white and red. An original set of works plates and newly cast number plates certainly made No.323 look different, but whether such embellishments, not to mention the new colours, met with the approval of the purists is open to question! Apparently *Bluebell*'s new brass nameplates failed to arrive on time, but a member skilfully painted her name on the tanksides.

Roy Denison

Lifting of the Ardingly to East Grinstead line, which excluded the immediate area of Horsted Keynes station, commenced in July 1964 starting at Ardingly and using a temporary base at West Hoathly. The contractors got off to a disastrous start when their small diesel locomotive failed on 15th July and they had to enlist assistance from the Bluebell who loaned one of their fleet, usually No.2650, the North London Railway 0-6-0T locomotive, or *Birch Grove*. Slow progress was made initially, apparently because the men experienced difficulty removing the third rail and its associated fittings and by 6th August they had only got as far as the first underline bridge beyond Ardingly. The lifting gang consisted of only two men and a crane driver, the lengths of track being lifted out bodily and transported to West Hoathly where another gang dismantled the track panels into their component parts. In this picture *Birch Grove* steams along between Ardingly and Horsted Keynes on a lovely day in September 1964.

Roy Hobbs

The death of a railway. There can be few more distressing sights for a railway enthusiast than that of a line being slowly erased from the landscape, perhaps after a bitter struggle by local people to retain the service for the benefit of the community. In this view, taken at the former West Hoathly goods yard on 2nd October 1964, the North London tank engine stands amidst piles of sleepers, track panels, rails and telegraph poles, all salvaged for possible further use elsewhere. At the time the largest market for such materials was the National Coal Board and considerable quantities were despatched to collieries in the West Midlands, whilst the conductor rails (salvaged from the Ardingly branch) went to blast furnaces in South Wales. Providing the motive power was a substantial commitment for the Bluebell which required an early start by the engine crew, the locomotive being booked 'off shed' at Sheffield Park at 7.00am. The engine normally returned coupled to the rear of the 5.25pm from Horsted Keynes. *R. C. Riley*

Locomotive failures usually delay trains and chaos reigns for a time until things are back to normal. But the failure of the contractor's Ruston and Hornsby diesel shunter, in July 1964, soon after track lifting had commenced, was probably one of the most well received locomotive failures ever! It provided the Bluebell with a golden opportunity to make some much-needed extra cash by hiring out a steam locomotive as a replacement, and was an unexpected bonus for photographers who were able to take pictures of a steam train north of Horsted Keynes once again. The disgraced diesel shunter stands beneath the remains of the footbridge at West Hoathly on 4th October 1964, with the North London tank engine also visible. The wagon immediately behind the diesel locomotive contains a garden shed which was apparently used as mobile messing accommodation.

John Beckett

The Bluebell Railway's operations during 1965 continued to be overshadowed by the desperate need to raise funds for the Line Purchase Scheme, and at the society's annual general meeting in late February it was stated that the railway was still £4,750 short of the outstanding £20,000 needed to secure the line. The railway continued to be hugely popular with the general public, however, and receipts in 1964 had been an all-time record which augured well for the future. One steady source of income for the railway during the winter of 1964/65 were, of course, hire charges for the North London tank locomotive No.2650 which continued working for the contractors who were demolishing the section of the line north of Horsted Keynes. The use of the railway's locomotive had apparently benefited the Bluebell's coffers to the tune of £1,500 by February 1965, a very substantial sum at that time. In this picture No.2650 is seen near Imberhorne Lane in February 1965. *John Beckett*

The GWR 'Dukedog' locomotive No.9017 remained in black livery for some time after its arrival on the Bluebell, but was restored during the winter of 1964/65 which involved repainting into original GWR green livery and renumbering 3217. The resplendent 'Dukedog' was brought back into service during a ceremony at Sheffield Park station on 13th June 1965, and the society's special guests naturally included the two gentlemen responsible for the fund which saved the locomotive from the scrapheap. During the proceedings the engine was formally named *Earl of Berkeley*. In this picture, taken in dull conditions on 4th July 1965, No.3217 emits a splendid smoke effect as it climbs Freshfield Bank with an afternoon train. *Alan Chandler*

Left, above: The Bluebell was always on the look out for vehicles worth preserving and on 21st September 1963 a party of members visited Lancing Carriage Works to see if any remaining LBSCR coaches were suitable candidates for preservation. Unfortunately, the only passenger-carrying carriages were beyond redemption, but the party were pleased to discover a LBSCR milk van which was in reasonable condition. Its running gear had suffered from prolonged exposure to the sea air and needed attention before it could be moved, but this problem was not insuperable. The van was subsequently purchased by a small consortium of members and made fit to travel. It arrived at the Bluebell with *Fenchurch* in May 1964 and had been restored externally by the time this picture was taken in October 1965. *R.C.Riley*

Left, below: One of the most impressive vehicles on the Bluebell Railway is DS291 which was built at Lancing Carriage Works in 1913 as an Inspection Saloon for the Directors of the LBSCR. It was numbered 60 in their series. The coach is mounted on two six-wheeled bogies, weighs 40 tons and is 63ft. 8in. long. The carriage interior consists of one large and one small saloon, both sumptuously decorated, which are tabled for the service of meals prepared in the large, well-equipped kitchen. The vehicle also has a toilet and washroom. The coach is elaborately panelled and has a splendidly decorative ceiling. In 1933 it was rebuilt by the Southern Railway who changed its number to 291S and undertook various alterations, including re-designing the sidelights (windows) and rebuilding the ends with corridor connections. By 1965 No.DS291 had become the last surviving LBSCR coach on the mainland (several remained in daily service on the Isle of Wight) and the Bluebell made strenuous efforts to secure its preservation. It was bought by a group of members and arrived at the railway on 4th August 1965. Unfortunately, by this time the Bluebell's rail link to the outside world had been lost and the coach had to come by road which was in itself a major, and extremely expensive, operation equivalent to the purchase price of the vehicle. This picture of the carriage was taken at Horsted Keynes in April 1966 and, judging by the areas of aluminium priming paint, was being cosmetically restored. Surprisingly for such a vintage vehicle, it was fitted with electric train heating equipment in addition to steam heating. Sadly, at the time of writing this splendid example of LBSCR craftsmanship requires considerable attention and consequently has not been seen in public for many years. *Roy Hobbs*

A charming scene at Horsted Keynes on 2nd September 1967 showing 'Terrier' No.72 *Fenchurch* simmering in the station prior to leaving with the 'Wealden Rambler'. The signalman has apparently come across to the platform to 'borrow' some coal for his fire : perhaps he was stocking up for the winter! The coach immediately behind the locomotive is SECR No.1061, a brake vehicle with an elevated guard's lookout, commonly known as a 'Birdcage'. This carriage was withdrawn in 1952 and converted to a service vehicle which involved the removal of many internal fittings, but at least the seats and partitions remained. It arrived on the Bluebell on 5th February 1962 and a considerable amount of work was necessary before it entered traffic in 1965, but even then it was not entirely restored internally. It was taken out of service in early 1976 and is yet to reappear in traffic. *R.C.Riley*

Left, above: This Southern Railway directional sign survived at Horsted Keynes for some years after the Bluebell took over the wall adjacent to the subway steps: it was photographed in September 1967. One wonders how many passengers ever travelled from Horsted Keynes to Hastings! *Roy Hobbs*

Left, below: Coach No.1050 is a quite remarkable vehicle with, perhaps, the most complicated history of any preserved carriage. The coach's ancestry can be traced back to about 1880 when the South Eastern Railway constructed two non-bogie coaches which were later spliced together by the Southern Railway on a long, non-standard underframe. The coach which resulted from this fascinating exercise was No.5546, a composite vehicle, which entered service in 1927. In 1943 it was downgraded to third class only, renumbered 1050, and fitted for push-pull working on branch lines in the West Country. This unique carriage was withdrawn in the early 1960s and arrived at the Bluebell Railway on 2nd May 1963. It is pictured at Sheffield Park in September 1967 looking very presentable following repainting. This was probably the last major attention it received, because the coach was taken out of service in the early 1970s for a complete overhaul and is still awaiting restoration. *R. C. Riley*

The county of Sussex is reputed to be the most thickly wooded in England and passengers travelling along the Bluebell Line are constantly reminded of this as they pass numerous woods and thickets. In the spring many of these are carpeted with bluebells which are a joy to behold. Lindfield Wood, located about three miles north of Sheffield Park is, perhaps, the largest woodland on the line. Here, SECR P Class 0-6-0T No.27 is seen coming out of Lindfield Wood with a train bound for Horsted Keynes sometime during the summer of 1968. Curiously, very few photographs taken during 1968 were submitted for inclusion in this album. Certainly, that year was not a very exciting one photographically on the Bluebell and the attention of many railway enthusiasts was focussed on the north of England where BR steam was finally being laid to rest. *Kevin McCormack*

A short two-coach train does not provide *Fenchurch* with a particularly challenging assignment, and the sprightly 'Terrier' is seen romping along with a southbound train near Freshfield Halt on 7th September 1968. The structure in the background is the erstwhile Town House Bridge. Six weeks after this picture was taken there was a short ceremony at Sheffield Park station at which the General Manager of the Bluebell Railway was presented by a BR representative with a commemorative parchment marking the purchase of the line for a total of £43,500. The colossal effort made to raise this sum had been thoroughly worthwhile – the Bluebell had finally won through. What a wonderful achievement! *Alan Chandler*

In this photograph, taken near the former Town House bridge, SECR P Class No.27 is seen propelling a Christmas special train formed of the Observation Car. This shot was taken in December 1968. This is clearly a most unusual method of operation which was probably only permitted under 'one engine in steam' arrangements. *John Beckett*

This most unusual view of Sheffield Park station and yard was taken in 1969 from the tender of the 'Dukedog' locomotive and shows how much space there was in the yard compared to today. The photographer was clearly 'well-in' with the driver! Locomotives such as *Blackmore Vale* and the BR Standard 9F had yet to arrive on the scene and the Bluebell was still mainly operated by small locomotives. *Fenchurch* stands in the down platform at the front of a train from Horsted Keynes, whilst the coach in the cattle dock appears to be Maunsell Brake Composite No.6575, which was undergoing restoration at the time. The rear of newly arrived BR Standard Class 4MT No.75027 can be discerned beyond the temporary extension to the engine shed which provided valuable additional covered accommodation for the locomotive fleet. A view today from the same vantage point would be rather different and the somewhat congested engine shed yard, locomotive works and roof of the buffet block would be the most prominent features. *Roy Hobbs*

In this superb planned shot, *Bluebell* is depicted climbing Freshfield Bank on 20th September 1969. It is amazing to think that diminutive 0-6-0T locomotives, originally designed for nothing more strenuous than shunting and light passenger duties, were the mainstay of the Bluebell's service for more than ten years and proved to be extremely reliable and economical performers. *Alan Chandler*

Another shot of No.323 *Bluebell*, this time taken on 5th October 1969. The P Class locomotive has passed over the bridge at the top of Freshfield Bank and drifts down towards Sheffield Park. The coaches are SECR No.1050 and the LNWR Observation Car. By this time the line purchase was no longer top of the Bluebell's agenda and thoughts were turning to the long-term preservation of the line's carriages, some of which were suffering badly due to constant exposure to the elements. A leaflet was produced to highlight the plight of the coaches and supporters were implored to save the railway's 'rotting stock'.

Alan Chandler

Three Arch Bridge, just south of Horsted Keynes, is one of the best-known landmarks on the Bluebell Railway. It is also one of the largest civil engineering works on the line, but back in May 1970, when this picture was taken, much of the structure was hidden by trees and saplings that had become firmly established on the side of the adjacent cuttings. Today this area is reasonably clear of lineside vegetation. Here, a southbound train, headed by *Bluebell* passes Three Arch Bridge with two SECR coaches and the LNWR Observation Car in tow. *Chris Gammell*

A Horsted Keynes to Sheffield Park train, hauled by No.473 *Birch Grove*, has just passed the top of Freshfield Bank and starts the long descent to Sheffield Park. This picture was taken on 12th July 1970. The first vehicle in the formation is, of course, the Observation Car, but the second coach may not be so easily recognised by some readers. It is a Caledonian Railway vehicle which was used on special trains in Scotland in the 1960s, and the Bluebell rescued it in 1969 when its future appeared to be in doubt. Its stay on Bluebell metals proved to be short-lived, however, because it returned to its native Scotland in 1974.

Chris Gammell

Photographed on the same day as the previous picture, *Birch Grove* glints in the evening sunshine as it approaches Town House bridge with a southbound train. The former Freshfield Halt is just out of sight around the curve. *Chris Gammell*

An especially interesting picture taken at Horsted Keynes on 2nd May 1970. During early 1967 Universal Pictures filmed 'I'll Never Forget Whatshisname' and for this purpose Bluebell Halt was converted into a ghost station and two Chesham coaches were painted white to resemble a ghost train. The Chesham set of coaches, which were no doubt thoroughly worn out by this time, then went into long-term storage and the vehicle in the worst condition of the four only narrowly escaped scrapping. In this shot part of a white-painted Chesham coach can be seen on the left, partially covered by a tarpaulin, and clearly exposure to the weather is taking a heavy toll. By the date of this picture the Bluebell had made a start on modifying the track layout, which had remained largely unchanged since 1935, and part of the connection from Platform 3 (as it then was) to the former down Ardingly line has already been taken out, but the diamond crossing is still *in situ*. *Chris Gammell*